MAKING MODELS FROM JUNK

Jan Morrow

Illustrated by Karen Tushingham

CONTENTS

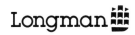

Longman

A message for young modellers

If you like to make models from Lego or bricks, you will enjoy using this book.

It will help you to make lots of exciting things from empty packets and boxes which are often thrown away.

If you have to use a knife or scissors, please ask a grown-up which are safe to use.

EGG BOX SPIDERS

YOU WILL NEED

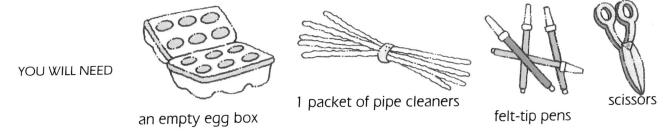

an empty egg box

1 packet of pipe cleaners

felt-tip pens

scissors

1

Cut out one of the egg box cups.

2

Ask a grown up to help you. Make eight small holes around the outside of the eggcup.

3

Use four pipe cleaners. Push each pipe cleaner through a hole in one side of the cup and out through a hole on the other side. Bend the pipe cleaners.

4

Draw a spider's face on the front of the egg cup.

EGG BOX GIRAFFE

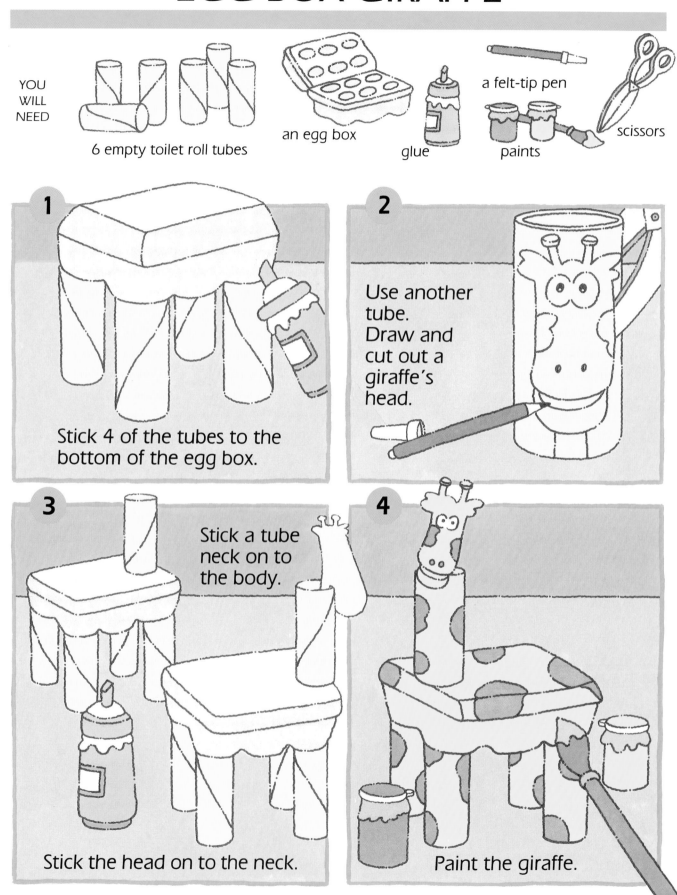

YOU WILL NEED

6 empty toilet roll tubes

an egg box

glue

a felt-tip pen

paints

scissors

1 Stick 4 of the tubes to the bottom of the egg box.

2 Use another tube. Draw and cut out a giraffe's head.

3 Stick a tube neck on to the body.

Stick the head on to the neck.

4 Paint the giraffe.

EGG BOX GOGGLES

YOU WILL NEED

an egg box

scissors

elastic

a stapler

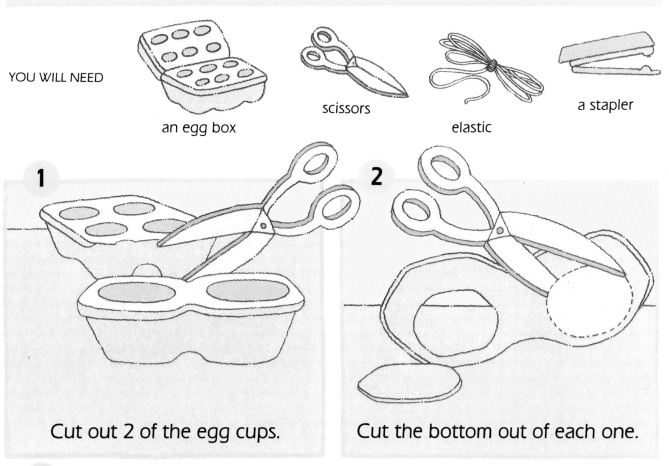

1 Cut out 2 of the egg cups.

2 Cut the bottom out of each one.

3 Staple some elastic to the goggles.

CATERPILLAR EGGBOX

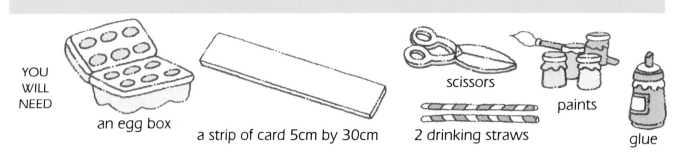

YOU WILL NEED

an egg box

a strip of card 5cm by 30cm

scissors

paints

2 drinking straws

glue

1 Use the scissors to cut out the egg box cups.

2 Paint the outside of the cups with pretty patterns.
On one of the cups paint a face.

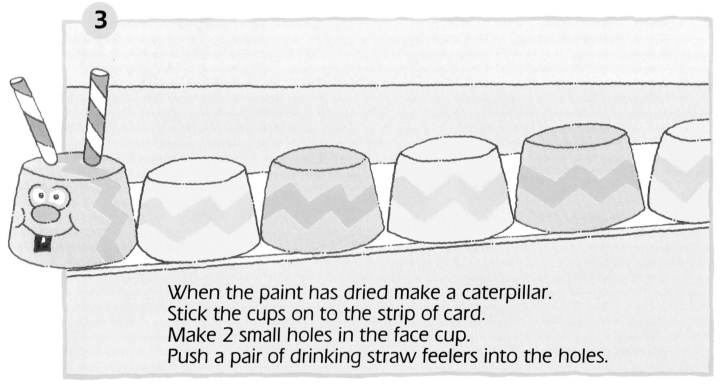

3 When the paint has dried make a caterpillar.
Stick the cups on to the strip of card.
Make 2 small holes in the face cup.
Push a pair of drinking straw feelers into the holes.

EGG BOX FLOWERS

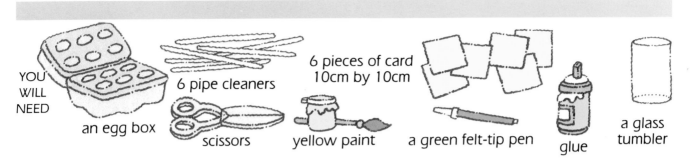

YOU WILL NEED

an egg box

6 pipe cleaners

scissors

yellow paint

6 pieces of card 10cm by 10cm

a green felt-tip pen

glue

a glass tumbler

1

Draw and cut out six flower shapes from the card.

Paint the shapes yellow.

2

Cut out the egg box cups and paint them yellow.

3

Glue the cups on to the flower shapes.

4

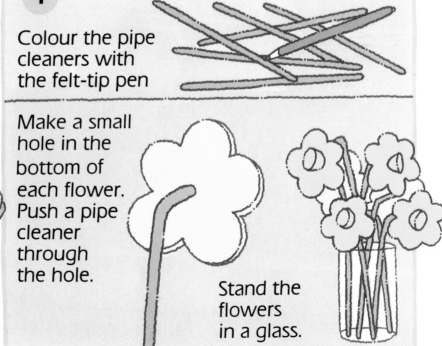

Colour the pipe cleaners with the felt-tip pen

Make a small hole in the bottom of each flower. Push a pipe cleaner through the hole.

Stand the flowers in a glass.

7

A GROCERY BOX TOTEM POLE

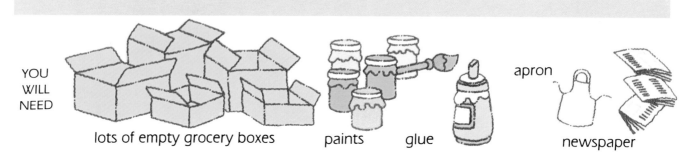

YOU WILL NEED

lots of empty grocery boxes   paints   glue   apron   newspaper

1 Cover the floor with newspaper.

2 Paint the boxes with patterns and faces.

3 Glue the boxes one on top of another until you have made a tall totem pole.

ROBOTS

YOU WILL NEED

a spray can of silver paint   lots of grocery boxes   clean milk bottle tops   tinfoil   scissors   glue

1 Ask a grown up to help you to spray the boxes with silver paint.

2 Make a robot with the boxes. Glue the boxes together.

3 Make a face on the robot by using the bottle tops and foil. Glue bottle tops on to the robot's body.

9

A DOLLS HOUSE

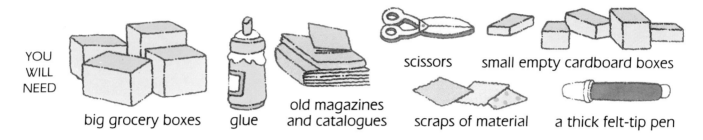

YOU WILL NEED

big grocery boxes · glue · old magazines and catalogues · scissors · small empty cardboard boxes · scraps of material · a thick felt-tip pen

1

Cut the tops off the big boxes.

Glue the boxes together.

2

Use the pen to draw doors and windows inside the boxes.

3

Cut out the pictures of furniture from the magazines. Glue the pictures on to the inside walls of the boxes.

4

Use the material to glue curtains on to the windows. Use the small boxes to make pretend furniture.

BOX CARS AND TRAINS

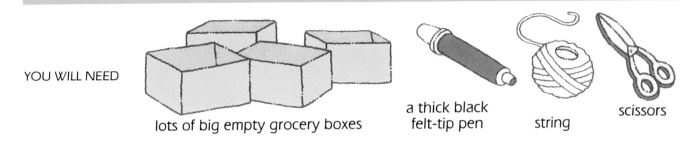

YOU WILL NEED

lots of big empty grocery boxes

a thick black felt-tip pen

string

scissors

1

To make a car.
Draw wheels, headlights, buttons and levers on the boxes with the felt-tip pen.

2

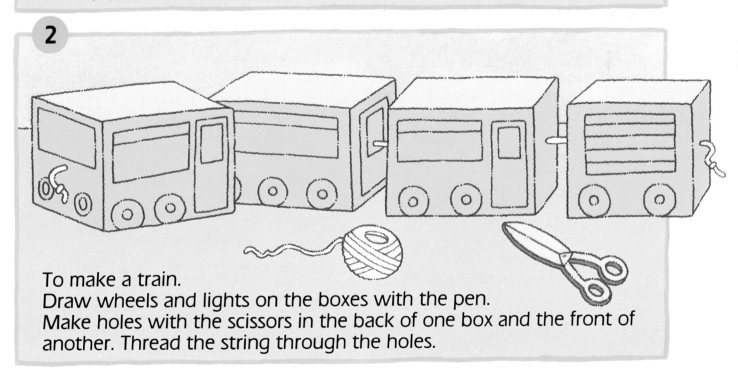

To make a train.
Draw wheels and lights on the boxes with the pen.
Make holes with the scissors in the back of one box and the front of another. Thread the string through the holes.

SPACE ROCKET

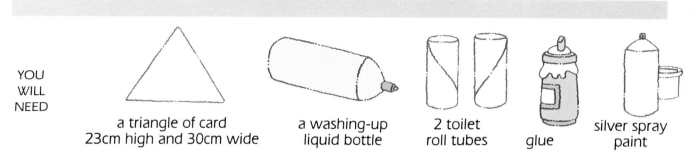

YOU WILL NEED

a triangle of card
23cm high and 30cm wide

a washing-up
liquid bottle

2 toilet
roll tubes

glue

silver spray
paint

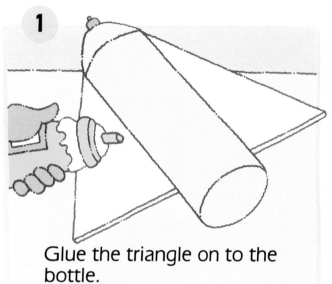

1 Glue the triangle on to the bottle.

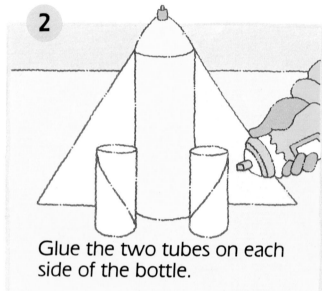

2 Glue the two tubes on each side of the bottle.

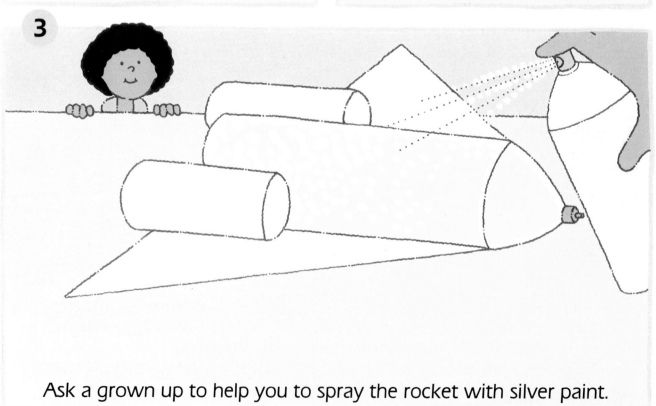

3 Ask a grown up to help you to spray the rocket with silver paint.

A LIGHTHOUSE

YOU WILL NEED

 a washing-up liquid bottle

 a plastic cottage cheese carton

 white emulsion paint

 a paint brush

 a felt-tip pen

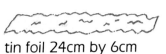 tin foil 24cm by 6cm

 glue   scissors

1

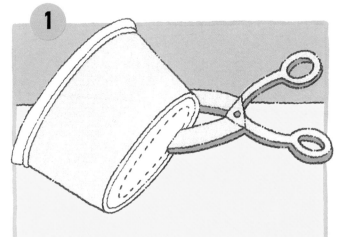

Cut a hole in the bottom of the cheese carton.

2

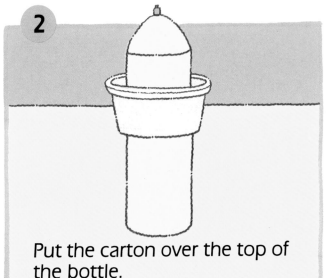

Put the carton over the top of the bottle.

3

Paint the lighthouse with the emulsion paint.

4

When the paint has dried, glue the foil round the top of the bottle.
Draw a door and windows on the lighthouse.

13

A PIGGY BANK

YOU WILL NEED

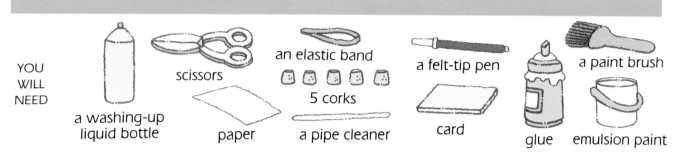

scissors

a washing-up liquid bottle

paper

an elastic band

5 corks

a pipe cleaner

a felt-tip pen

card

glue

a paint brush

emulsion paint

1

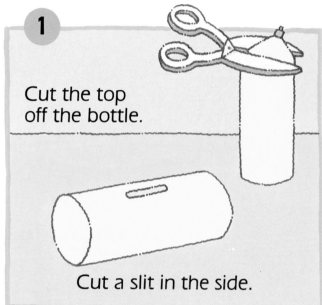

Cut the top off the bottle.

Cut a slit in the side.

2

Paint the bottle.

3

When the bottle has dried, cut out a paper circle and put it over the top of the bottle. Hold the paper on the bottle with the elastic band.

4

Make your piggy bank.

pipe cleaner tail

card ears

cork nose

cork legs

Draw a happy face on to the paper.

14

BANGLES

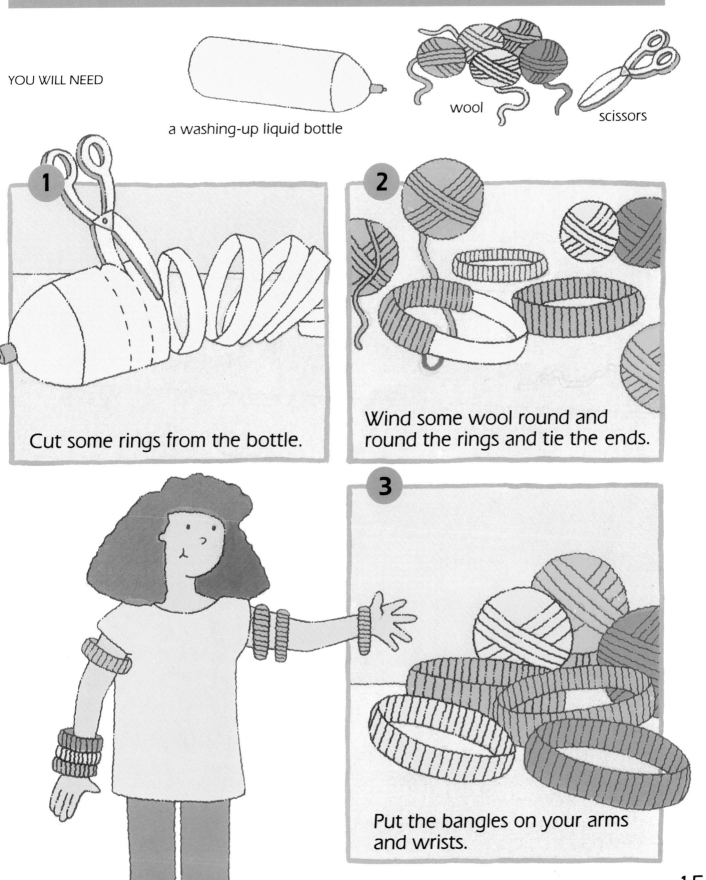

YOU WILL NEED

a washing-up liquid bottle

wool

scissors

1 Cut some rings from the bottle.

2 Wind some wool round and round the rings and tie the ends.

3 Put the bangles on your arms and wrists.

15

SKITTLES

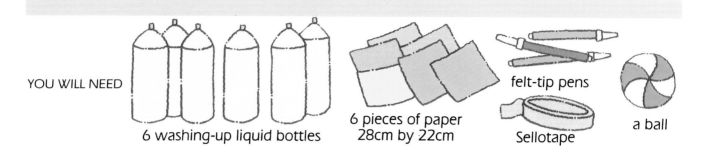

YOU WILL NEED

6 washing-up liquid bottles

6 pieces of paper 28cm by 22cm

felt-tip pens

Sellotape

a ball

1 Cover each bottle with paper. Sellotape the paper so that it doesn't fall off.

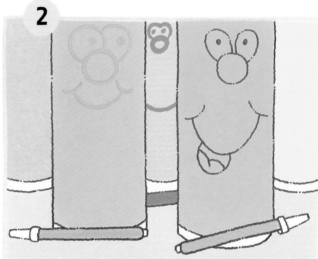

2 Draw some happy faces on the bottles.

3 Stand the bottles together. Stand six paces away and see how many you can knock down with the ball.

RAGGY DOGS

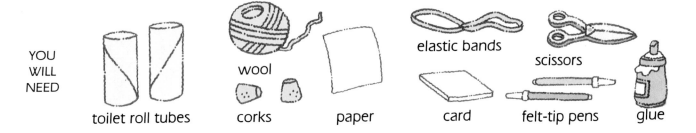

YOU WILL NEED

toilet roll tubes   wool   corks   paper   elastic bands   card   scissors   felt-tip pens   glue

1

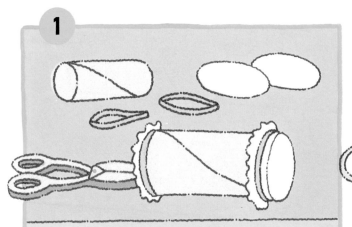

Cover both ends of a tube
with circles of paper.
Hold the paper on the tube
with the elastic bands.

2

Put some glue on the tube.
Cover the tube with long
strips of wool.

3

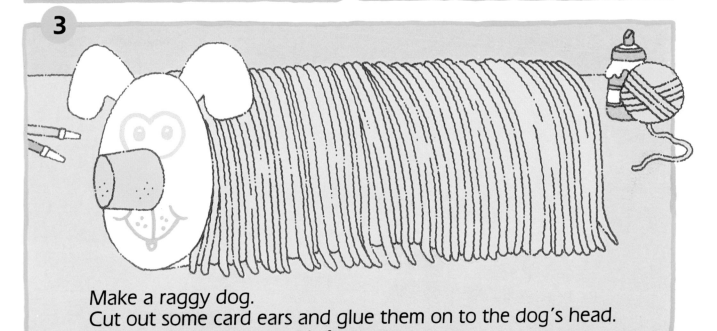

Make a raggy dog.
Cut out some card ears and glue them on to the dog's head.
Glue a cork nose on to his face.
Draw two eyes and a happy mouth.

A DESK TIDY

YOU WILL NEED

3 toilet roll tubes

3 sheets of pretty paper 17cm by 24cm

a sheet of card 15cm by 15cm

glue

Sellotape

1

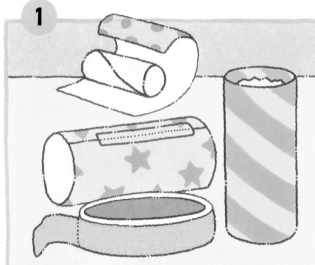

Wrap the paper round the tubes.
Sellotape the paper so that it doesn't fall off.
Tuck the loose ends of the paper inside the top and bottom of the tubes.

2

Glue one end of each tube. Press the tubes down on to the sheet of card.

3

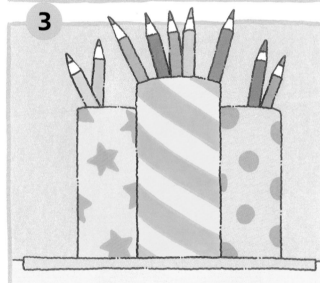

When the glue has dried you can stand your pens and pencils in the tubes.

TOY FARM

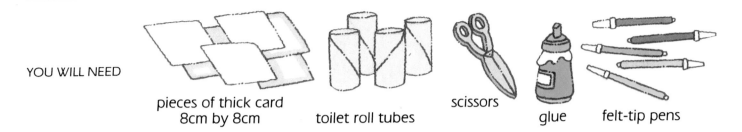

pieces of thick card
8cm by 8cm

toilet roll tubes

scissors

glue

felt-tip pens

1

Draw the front end of a farm animal on a piece of card.
Draw the back end of the animal on another piece of card.

2

Cut out the animals and stick them across the ends of a tube, with
the head at one end and the tail at the other.

BINOCULARS

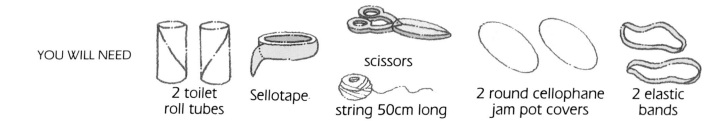

YOU WILL NEED

2 toilet roll tubes | Sellotape | scissors | string 50cm long | 2 round cellophane jam pot covers | 2 elastic bands

1

Put a jam pot cover over the end of each tube.
Push an elastic band round each tube to stop the cellophane from slipping off.

2

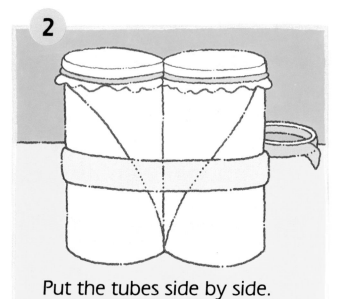

Put the tubes side by side.
Wrap some Sellotape around them.

3

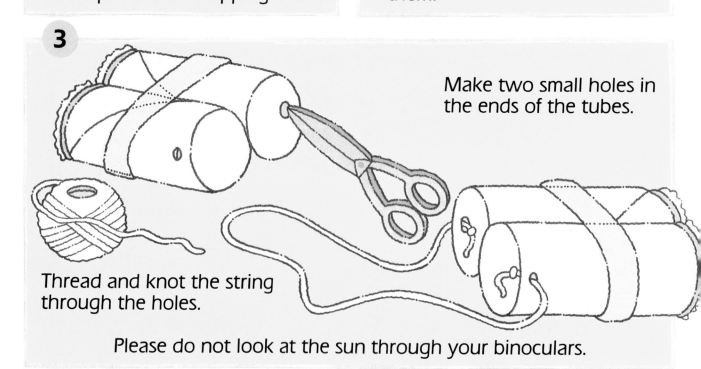

Make two small holes in the ends of the tubes.

Thread and knot the string through the holes.

Please do not look at the sun through your binoculars.

A CEREAL BOX TELEVISION

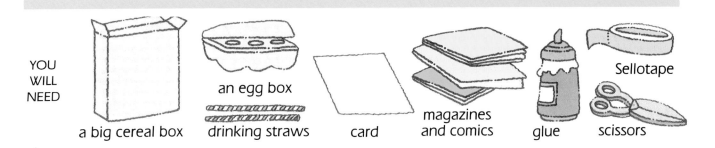

YOU WILL NEED

a big cereal box   an egg box   drinking straws   card   magazines and comics   glue   Sellotape   scissors

1

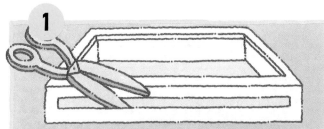

Cut out a rectangular hole from the front of the box.
Make a thin slit in the bottom.

2

Glue a colourful picture inside the box so that you can see it through the hole in the front.

3

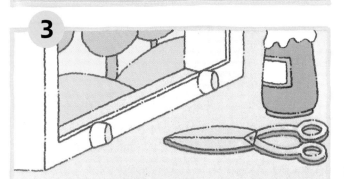

Cut out and glue 2 egg box cups on to the front of the television.

4

Cut out some animals and people from the magazines.
Glue these on to card.
When they are dry, cut them out.
Stick a straw on to the back of each one with Sellotape.

5

Pop the animals and people through the slit in the bottom of the box.

21

A SHOE BOX PEEP SHOW

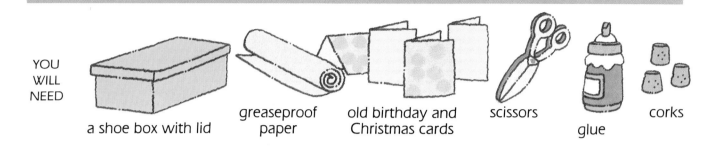

YOU WILL NEED

a shoe box with lid

greaseproof paper

old birthday and Christmas cards

scissors

glue

corks

1

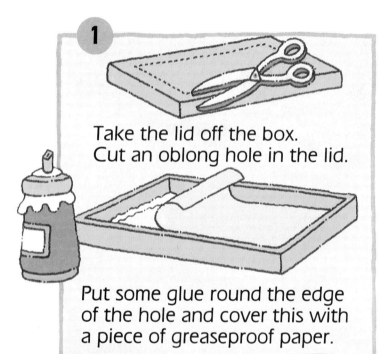

Take the lid off the box.
Cut an oblong hole in the lid.

Put some glue round the edge of the hole and cover this with a piece of greaseproof paper.

2

Glue a card picture inside the box.

3

Cut out people or animals from the cards.
Glue a cork on to the back of each cut out shape.
Glue the corks inside the box.

4

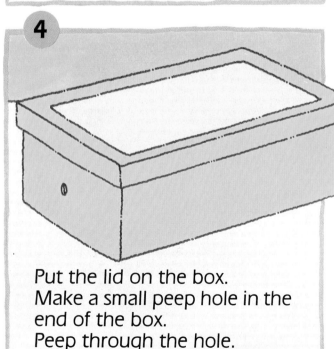

Put the lid on the box.
Make a small peep hole in the end of the box.
Peep through the hole.

TOY TOWN

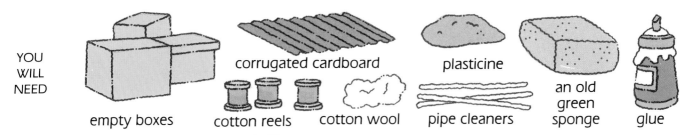

YOU WILL NEED

empty boxes · corrugated cardboard · cotton reels · cotton wool · plasticine · pipe cleaners · an old green sponge · glue

1

To make a box house.
Use a cotton reel and cotton wool to make a chimney and smoke.
Bend some corrugated cardboard for the roof.
Paint windows and doors on the box.

2

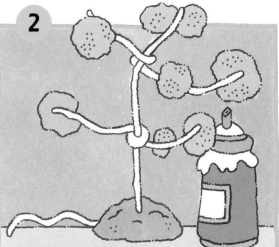

To make trees.
Twist pipe cleaners into tree shapes.
Glue small pieces of sponge on to the branches.
Stand the tree in plasticine.

3

To make a garage.
Cut a garage door from the side of a shoe box.

Paint the shoe box with garage signs. Use small boxes for petrol pumps.

GUITAR

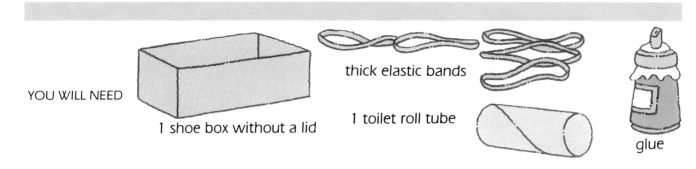

YOU WILL NEED

1 shoe box without a lid

thick elastic bands

1 toilet roll tube

glue

1

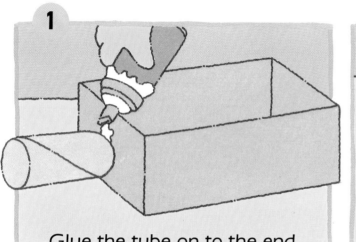

Glue the tube on to the end of the shoe box.

2

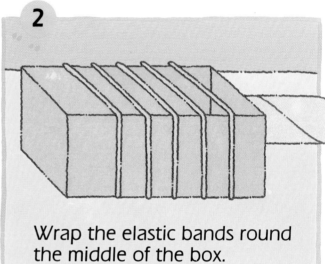

Wrap the elastic bands round the middle of the box.

3

When the glue has dried you can play your guitar.